Great True Stories to Read Aloud

By Dennis Shives

D1564496

Meadow Dancer Press
Ojai, California

My other books are **"True Stories to Read Aloud"** by Dennis Shives and **"More True Stories to Read Aloud"** by Dennis Shives. Both books are available on Amazon.

CONTENTS

ACKNOWLEDGMENTS

This book is dedicated to the memory of the late Allen Rains, who would accompany me around to the local hospitals and rest homes to read stories to people who needed a little lift. Allen was a great human being.

Also, special thanks to Christopher Wehling for editing and arranging my stories.

Finally, to my friend and life partner, Laurie Edgcomb, I give not just my warmest thanks but also my heart.

PREFACE

I write these stories now so someday when I can't remember anything, I can read them and think, wow, the guy that wrote this must've lived a pretty fun life...I wish I knew him.

Mule Skinner

Now just to set things straight first, mule skinners do not skin mules. Mule skinners are usually cowboys that learned how to ride horses, and then over time they realized how much smarter mules are then horses. Now if you are settled and of the right temperament, you might be lucky enough to have a great mule train you. And after a while, if you understand how they think and work, maybe they will let you become a mule skinner.

I have a handful of friends that are mule skinners. I was visiting one of them a while back when he told me he was getting ready to take a load of supplies up the mountain to a tent camp. It was the last run for the summer season and my friend asked if I wanted to ride along. He needed someone on the back mule to keep things moving in the rear of the pack train. I was just about ready to head south for the winter, but one last ride sounded like fun.

We spent several hours harnessing and loading up the mules. Finally, at about noon, we got on and headed up the trail. Once we were out of the lower canyons and started gaining altitude, the views became spectacular . The mules were moving along well but we stopped every so often to check the pack saddles. We didn't want any sores from rubbing. You've got to keep mules happy, you know.

When we stopped in the middle of the afternoon to eat, I could hear what sounded like gunfire in the distance. The mule skinner said it was bighorn sheep banging heads. As we got a little closer, I could see them. They would rise up on their back feet and charge, banging horns. It took about five seconds for the sound to reach us.

We were making good time, feeling great, telling stories as we started up a steeper, narrower section of trail. It was headed around a long, slow, outside curve in the middle of an avalanche shoot. The trail was only about a foot wide, and the angle of the terrain was really steep. We quit talking so as not to distract the mules. Then we heard a rock fall up ahead, and we stopped the mule train. As we sat there listening, a large pair of ears came into view. Then a whole mule with another mule skinner on it. And then another fully loaded mule train with ten mules came into view. Sixteen mules with six-foot wide packs and four skinners stood facing each other on a one foot wide trail with no place to turn around.

I started to get off when my skinner said, "Stay on, let the mules take care of this. Think good thoughts, and if it's too scary, close your eyes. If you get off, the mules will think you don't believe in them." I couldn't watch so I closed my eyes. We just sat there for a few minutes. There were rocks falling and leather squeaking and mule grunting going on. Then finally we started to move and I opened my eyes. The down hill mules had climbed up the steep hillside and stood there, while the uphill mules slowly picked their way by. The packs never touched. The mules knew exactly how much room they needed. I think if I had gotten off I would have fallen all the way down the mountain. It was so steep. It seemed like forever but it only took a few minutes for those twenty mules to safely pass each other, and soon we were on our way.

If I live to be a hundred years old, I will never forget that experience. It was the most wonderful showing of animal intelligence and kindness I ever saw. For a few minutes it felt like I was a mule skinner too.

Something else I learned from them that day: when you run into trouble in life, trust your mule.

Scratches

Whenever I feel like thinking in a new direction, I just go out and follow a bear trail. Bears are free of all the low cost/high profit ideas of modern man. They just stick to the basics: food, water, love, and sleep. They know the shortest, easiest ways to get to what they want. The schedules of the trash trucks, when and where the wild berries are ripe, and where the windfall avocados are softening in the morning sun. They know where you keep the dog food. They can take the peel off a pixie tangerine in one piece. They even know where the water pipe is leaking for a quick drink on a hot day. Bears are amazing people.

I was climbing a small creek the other day, looking for something exciting and stumbled upon an old bear trail across the creek from the people trail. The tracks were two inches deep and sixteen inches apart. The bears had been stepping in each other's tracks for many years. It made it hard to walk on their trail. I got off to one side and followed them up the hill. The path led off through the brush away from the river. I ducked under low branches as I moved along. I came out in a small clearing off to the side of an access road. I followed the trail up to a curved oak tree that seemed to please the bears. There were no low branches and the trunk was shiny from all the rubbing it had received over the years. I leaned down and took a sniff. Wow what a stench, someone had found something remarkable to roll in. I'm sure the other bears were envious. I turned and followed the sunken bear tracks across the service road and back into the brush again.

The tracks weaved around through the chaparral, finally coming out in another clearing near a bend in the river. There was an oak tree growing in a spot that was close enough to the river for the roots to get a drink. Being so big it was safe from most fires because nothing could grow in it's shade. The trunk was nearly six feet across, making it between four and five hundred years old. It was a huge tree. As I got closer I noticed scratch marks, lots of scratch marks. They started about four feet and went to about eight feet high all the way around the base of the tree. I circled it a couple of times admiring the claw marks and bites.

I could see where the bigger bears had chewed the bottoms of the low limbs. About the third time around, I happened to look up a little higher on the back side of the trunk and saw bigger, wider scratch marks. Some of them looked very old. They were ten feet high, two feet higher than all the new scratches. These scratches were so much higher and older than the others, that they had to be California grizzly bear claw marks, from the 1800's or before. I was blown away!

Sneaky Scoundrels

I don't remember whose idea it was, but it sounded like fun. Let's see if we can sneak into the fair and play music in the middle of the day on Saturday. We filled my old VW van with amplifiers, drums, and dressed up really nice. Then with another car behind us, full of finger pickers and guitars, we pulled up to the back gate (where the 4H kids get in).

We told the security that we were supposed to play at 1:30 PM on the back stage (where they showed and judged small animals.) The guys looked at each other, shrugged their shoulders and opened the gate. What a thrill, we were in! We drove slowly around, through the big crowds and backed up to the stage, hauled out all our stuff and began setting up. There were a few chicken cages in the way but they were quickly removed by some helpful 4H kids. It was so kind of them to help us sneaky scoundrels.

We got everything set up and ready to start before realizing we forgot to bring an extension cord. I made a quick pass through the chicken building and lifted a cord from the incubator. It was a warm summer day and I thought it would be ok (the chicks were all hatched). When I got back to the band, a cheer went up and I plugged us in. We started off with a country song, 'Mama don't let your babies grow up to be cowboys' and pulled up a pretty good crowd. We had ourselves an instant party with everybody singing and dancing. The beer booth loved us.

We wanged around for a good hour and a half before some guy in a tall cowboy hat with a big fancy buckle reached over and pulled our stolen chicken incubator cord out of the wall.

Then he told us to get our stuff off the stage and out of the fair grounds. I think it was one of my favorite musical experiences and I sure hope none of you young bucks try to copy us sneaky scoundrels…

P.S. I put the cord back on the incubator.

Through the Top

It's been pouring rain with a big Pacific storm pounding the coast . I'm sitting at the galley table in the cabin of the Rama Lee, listening. I have just returned from California for another summer in Alaska. As cold and miserable as it is, I am still thrilled to be back in the far north. The boat is tied off to a dock in the Seward Harbor, and I can see salmon jumping on their way up the river nearby to spawn. Inside the oil stove is dripping burning diesel for heat.

I need to get out and move around. I'm tired of just sitting. I put on my rain gear and headed into town to get some breakfast at a restaurant near the end of the dock. When I get close, there is a line to get in so I join it. It looks like the food is pretty good. While I'm waiting, I notice an enclosed glass case on the wall with old pictures in it. Reading the descriptions under the pictures I realize they were taken after the earthquake in 1964, when the whole town was wiped out. Two men walked up and got in line behind me. They looked like local fishermen so I asked them about the pictures and to my surprise they said," We were there."

The two men told me the story. It was around Easter 1964. They left the harbor in a fishing boat headed for Kodiak Island, and they were on the water so we didn't feel the actual earthquake. The Coast Guard warned all boats that there might be a tsunami coming (tidal wave), so they headed down Resurrection Bay at full throttle (8 mph). They said, "At first it was hard to see the wave but as it moved into shallower water it began to rise."

The narrowing of the bay made it rise even more. Soon it was crashing through the spruce trees on either side of the inlet. As the fisherman's boat rose higher and higher up the wave, they could see over the hills into the next valley. They said the tidal wave got steeper and began to curl over them. They were still 50 feet from the top when the wave finally broke and covered the little fishing boat. The water out the windows got darker and darker green, and they thought they were goners. They could hear the smoke stack exhaust pipe bubbling as they chugged down deeper. Then the green water got lighter and lighter and they popped through the top of the 150 foot high breaking Tsunami. The wave smashed down Resurrection Bay and completely destroyed the city of Seward, Alaska.

I bought my new friends breakfast and thanked them for the great story. It was still raining though. When I got back to the boat, Captain Jack was ready to go. I looked down the bay and the ocean didn't look any better than before, but Jack being the eternal optimist that he was, said it's ok, it's declining. It had gone from 25 foot seas to 24 foot seas and we headed off for Homer. About half way back we pulled into the relatively calm water of the windy bay and I dreamed about tidal waves all night long!

Emma May

I was one of those fortunate people that had a grandmother. There is only one more fortunate group, and that is those who have grandmothers that are artists. I was one of those too!

Her friends called her the church mouse. She was a church secretary most of her life. She would drag me to church every sunday with hopes of me being saved, but it didn't work. When she gave me money to tithe with, I'd sneak downtown and buy candy and MAD magazines to read in the back row. She recognized my talents at a very early age and gave me acrylic paints, brushes and canvas to work with. She told all her friends how talented I was, and made me feel good about myself through those tough early years. She gave me art. I wasn't the sterling little boy she wished I was, but she never gave up on me.

Her house always smelled like turpentine and oil paint. She painted beautiful land and seascapes. She wasn't very big, but she knew who she was and stuck up for herself. Actually she was a very beautiful woman but she didn't like using her personal charms to get what she wanted. She was brought up in South Dakota, in a good family, with a big farm where they raised chickens and grew corn and wheat for their animal feed business . They had an old Chinese man working for them that could tell a hen from a rooster by holding the egg up to a candle. He saved them a lot of money. She had four brothers and when they had disagreements her father would give them boxing gloves and lock them in the basement until they settled the problem. Her two sisters were also artists. Florence was married to Arthur Larson, a road scholar who became the Deputy Secretary Of Labor and wrote all of president Eisenhower's speeches. He also wrote all the workers' compensation laws and legislation. Her sister Florence was a sculptor. She made beautiful realistic marble statues of people and animals, and painted in oils. Emma May's other sister Doris was the Secretary of Labor for the state of Florida, who lived in Key West and was a great oil painter as well. Teal Rowe, who had grandparents that were both artists, heard me talking about my grandmother one day. Teal said,"You have a grandmother that teaches art in Santa Barbara and you aren't in her class, what's the matter with you!"

We both started going every Thursday from 1:00 to 4:00pm at Presidio Springs Senior Center. Many of my friends went too. My grandma taught there for twenty-two years. She was the oldest person in California to receive an art grant at 89 years old.

When I painted in her class, some of the other students would come and watch me and never say a word. They were painting from photographs. My pictures were stories: *The Last Supper* with bears in a cave at a big table eating fish, or *The Door To The Unknown*, slightly open with a prism light shining under it, or *Sing For Your Supper*, coyotes sitting on a rock singing in the moonlight to a field full of rabbits. My grandmother loved all of them. She was proud of me, she helped me believe in myself.

Thank you grandma, I really miss you......and special thanks to Teal also.

A Blessing of the Angels

It was 5 o'clock on Sunday afternoon and I was rolling along I-90 headed west towards the Emerald City of Seattle. I had been visiting old friends in Joseph, Oregon for a big part of the summer. I wanted to see my brother and his wife before heading down the coast to make a few sand sculpture festivals on my way back home. As I drove over the top of the Cascades and started down the hill, I was worried about traffic. There was always a lot coming back into the city after a late summer weekend.

The last time I came to Seattle, it was raining and dark. The reflections of all the tail lights on the wet, five lane highway made driving a real adventure. Then all the traffic stopped. It took me hours to finally get to their house. This time I hoped to get there before dark.

Coming down the rolling hills east of the city, I noticed the normally crowded freeway was nearly empty. The closer I got, the road traffic completely disappeared and I was the only car on the entire ten lanes of thorofare. It was sort of spooky like a B movie. I was in my old VW van putting down this giant empty freeway, going about 40 miles per hour, looking around at all the houses. I kept expecting it to change, but it never did. I drove all the way to Lake Washington. Through the tunnels I remember being passed by only one pickup truck, a gardener with lawn mowers and rakes in the back. I was shocked at how nice it was to have the entire freeway to myself.

I almost made it to I-5 before I ran into any traffic. It was almost 20 miles of being the only guy on the road. As I got on the main road, traffic picked up but I only had a short way to go before my turn to southwest Seattle and up the hill to my brother's house. I parked my van and went up to the door and knocked. They welcomed me and invited me in, just in time for dinner. After dinner, I told them about my eazy drive into town and they laughed. My brother told me there had been a Blue Angels air show over the city and they had shut down the freeway for a couple of hours. I must have been the first car down the hill after they opened the road. I told my brother, it was a wonderful welcome to the city of Seattle that I shall never forget.

And I would love to personally thank the angels.

The Swimming Hole

It was summertime in upper Ojai. I was going into fifth grade at Summit School, gainfully employed picking apricots on the Hall ranch. I felt good about myself. I would pick an apricot and eat it, then pick one and put it in my bucket. We weren't getting paid much, so I loaded up on fruit. This was before my old friend Terry Lutts father, "Hub", built the swimming pool on Topa Topa lane.

My brother and I would go up to Sesar Creek and work on the dam for our own swimming hole. Every time we did, the water got a little deeper. By the end of August, the pool was fifty feet long and five feet deep in places, and we could dive in and swim. It was lovely out in the country back then, but lonely. At least we had a place to swim. On the weekends people were home and the place was a little more lively.

One Saturday when my brother was gone into town, I decided to go swim by myself. It was hot and my feet were burning as I ran towards the swimming hole, I noticed fresh tracks on the path. When I got closer to the creek I stopped and listened .I could hear girls talking and laughing, I slowed down, snuck up close to the water and got down behind the sage.

There were five naked women swimming in our pond, laughing and splashing each other in the bright sunlight, and they were beautiful. I felt like running away but my feet wouldn't go. It was such a wonderful sight, I just sat there and watched. Finally, I heard my brother calling me. It was all I could do to leave. I quietly crawled away then stood up and ran home. My brother saw me coming and said, "Why are you running so fast!"

"It's the greatest thing you ever saw " I told him. "Beautiful grown up girls are swimming nude in our pond, come on!" We ran back up the trail and listened but they were already gone. (My brother believed me because the rocks were still wet).

Many years later I told one of the women swimming that day my story. "You were so beautiful, it was the most wonderful sight a young boy could ever see." She smiled at me, then laughed and said,

"Thank you for reminding me that I was pretty, you made my day!"

The Vampire train

At the end of October, I was driving back home from my early morning bear watching hike. I noticed strange beings crossing the road ahead. I slowed way down so as to not hurt anything.

I found myself stopped in front of the Monica Ros school to let a tiny squad of stormtroopers cross the road. (For some reason I thought they were bigger than that.) Right behind them a fairy princess, two mermaids and pirates also crossed in front of me. The whole street seemed to be full of ghosts and goblins, right there in broad daylight. Then a ballerina and a baby dragon happened by, and I thought I had better pull over to park and see what in the world was going on. I didn't realize they sent young dragons to school. It seems like breathing fire might be a little disruptive in class.

I got out of my van and walked over to the school's main gate. As I walked past the sand box, I ran into what appeared to be a miniature monster parade. There were football players, super heros and future farmers moving by. I glanced over my shoulder and thought I saw Harry Potter! It finally dawned on me that it must be Halloween!

I followed the parade around the corner onto the commons behind the blue room. Everyone had gathered in a big circle on the lawn. Then out of the strange and wonderful crowd stepped Susan, the headmaster of the school. She was dressed up like a cowgirl, and carried a microphone. She walked around the middle of the circle and admired all the costumes for a few moments,and then she stopped. Standing right in front of her was a handsome young boy in an engineer's hat, wearing a beautifully made, cardboard old fashioned train engine. His head and shoulders were sticking out in the middle, the place where they put sand for the brakes. The boy was chomping a pair of purple vampire teeth.

Without missing a beat, Susan said, "Will all the vampire trains please come out so we can see them?" Susan took his hand and walked him around the circle. When they had completed their loop, Susan let go of his hand and asked all the superheroes to please come out. Well the vampire train thought he fit pretty good in that category too, so he followed them around. It's amazing what a little recognition will do. He was easy to spot in that train outfit and he just kept on circling. The last time I looked , he was making the loop with those three fairies, still chomping those purple vampire teeth.

Popcorn

Dunnings Lagoon near Red mountain, across the Kachemak bay from Homer, Alaska, had many lessons for me. I loved to sit in the quiet of the morning drinking coffee, watching the tidal river sweep by. There was a resident sea otter and a crazy wonderful loon that washed through nearly everyday. They didn't swim around much, They just dove down and came up catching food. The tide would carry them all the way to the head of the bay. When I stopped for lunch I would notice them sailing away down the bay on the ebbing tide.

One day a local man came by and asked if I would like to see the eagle chicks being raised on the top of a rock outcropping a little ways up the bay. I said "Sure let's go!"

I got in his skif and we motored slowly along, looking for wildlife along the way. We passed over a big red octopus and when she saw us, she turned pure white and swished away. Soon enough we could see the big stone outcropping with two fuzzy eagle chicks watching us approach. The little poodle dog my friend brought along (named for what he looked like, Popcorn) began to get all excited. As our skif drifted over and bumped the rock, he jumped out and ran towards the chicks. Almost immediately we heard the screams of an angry pair of eagles. They were so far away that all we could see were two tiny white specks. Taking off from a tall spruce snag over a mile down the lagoon, here the eagles came like rocket ships!

Dave started yelling, "Popcorn come here,...come here, Popcorn!" The little poodle ran around the terrified eagle chicks a couple of more times barking and headed back towards the boat in no big hurry. Then the approaching parents screamed again,

Popcorn came running. He jumped for the skiff and the first eagles claws missed him by a whisker! I felt the wind as they sailed over me. We backed away from the rock and hightailed it back down the bay with one very lucky dog…

Caught

When building monsters, you want a big visual impact. Old Hoover, the monster of Lake Casitas had it. She was my third parade float! Forty feet long, fourteen feet high and ten feet wide, I had to drive her to the parade (she was far too big to haul).

The machine under the fish was powered by a VW engine and transaxle mounted in front with rear wheel steering . It gave the fish a believable look as it swam down the parade route. The huge mouth opened and closed threatening any close bystanders. When the gills opened the duel bubble machines kicked on, throwing out clouds of bubbles to help drive the children wild.

All the moving parts were powered by an air compressor mounted on top of the engine, with an air tank. Hoses went to tire pumps with bungee cords to give back and forth action. There was a seat up high above the engine,where special friends were invited to run the animation during parades. There was a big old fashioned air pressure gauge that looked like it came from the steampunk era, and lots of levers that made everything go, including the swish of the tail. Getting to sit up there made you feel like the Wizard of Oz!

It was always a thrill to trip check my monster the morning before heading off to a parade. Gas, oil, belts, air pressure in the tires, leaks in the air movement hose systems, and don't forget to fill the bubble machines!

The monster fish went to every parade in the county. I even drove it to Santa Barbara at the last moment to enter the fiesta parade, but they wouldn't let us in because they thought it might scare the horses. It was great fun for me just driving it up there and back. I could hear people at the lake screaming and yelling as we motored by.

Driving to the parades was usually wilder than the parades. No one expected to see a forty foot fish on the highway and people were blown away. Young kids screamed ,grown ups yelled and honked their horns at us as we went by. One time when I started over the old two-lane bridge across the Santa Clara river, I heard the field workers holler "piscado grandy." Moving that fish around was a noisy business.

It was always amazing to see people's reactions at the parades. Families would be sitting in chairs and I would come down the street in a fourteen foot high monster fish with big colorful lures in her lips and fins. I could see out through the painted skin cover but you couldn't see in. I gave everybody a cloud of bubbles and a swish from my tail as I swam down the street, trying to catch a frog on a bicycle leaving a trail of bubbles from the wind powered bubble machine. We left everyone standing up yelling, "look at that!" The parents had to hold on to their kids to keep them from chasing me down the street. We all had a good time.

One year at the Camarillo Christmas parade, I stayed longer than I should have. The days are short in December and I was talking and taking kids for rides in the fish. By the time I got going it was getting late. It was a long drive home and I had to pull over a lot to let traffic go by. I had a lead car with lights but I noticed it was getting pretty dark. Then the whole inside of the fish turned a lovely shade of red. I thought I might be on fire so I pulled over and looked back to see what was going on. The police were literally right on my tail! Old Hoover, the one that always got away, was caught. The officer walked up to the front of the fish and said something I couldn't understand. I said "I'm way back here officer."

He walked back near where I was sitting and asked if I had any tail lights. I told him no, and tried to explain how I left too late from the Christmas parade in Camarillo and ran out of daylight. He thought for a long moment and said, "Merry Christmas I will follow you home."

All I could say was, "Merry Christmas to you too and thank you sooo much!"

The Blubber Shark

Thinking back now, why we went fishing in the middle of the night, in a borrowed ski boat, five miles out in the ocean, is beyond me. It was 10:00 PM when we cleared the brakewake water and opened up the throttle, flying over the smooth night sea. We headed out to the first oil platform leaving behind us a sparkling biophosferesent trail in the pale moonlight. After about thirty minutes of full throttle, we slowed down as we approached the huge hollow steel pilings that support the giant oil drilling platform. The clearance lights were on, shining down on us but there was nobody home. The lights made it a little less spooky to be so far out in the ocean and in a few minutes we had our fishing poles baited and in the water. The fishing was great and soon we had caught more than we could keep so my friend started cleaning fish as I packed them in ice chests. As he finished each fish he threw them over the side into the deep dark ocean below. I was mezzmerized by the disappearing fish. I could see them for a long time as they slowly twirled downward with the light from above.

Then I remember feeling the boat lift. The sea was flat and calm so it surprised me. As I looked over the side, a beautiful round sweeping curve slowly emerged from the shadow of the boat. It got wider and wider until it was nearly six feet across and then gradually began to thin back down as it moved out into the lights of the platform above us. Then I could see the huge pectoral fins coming out of the sides underneath. It was eating the fish we were throwing over the side. When the tail finally came out and into view the huge fish gracefully turned and swam along the side of our tiny little boat. It's massive dorsal fin came out of the water. It was a great big white shark. Our boat measured about sixteen feet and this fish was at least four feet longer.

We both stopped and watched this fish circle us in complete silence for a long time, maybe four or five passes. We had stopped feeding her and she looked like she wanted to come up and see what was happening. I started the motor on our boat which now felt like a small inner tube and eazed away from the huge shark. I remember thinking, motor don't fail me now.

We made it back to the dock, tied up and unloaded our fish. We looked at each other and said, can you believe that happened?

We told our story to an old fisherman on the dock and he told us that those big sharks never come close to the shore. They mostly feed on floating dead whales. They're called blubber shark's, and we had ourselves a good laugh. I'm so thankful we didn't catch her, she may have knocked the oil platform over.

The Second Floor

My old friend Snow Deer was all lit up one morning when I stopped by. A humming bird was building a nest right next to her bedroom window. As the nest neared completion, a eucalyptus leaf from a tree close by, came twirling down and landed point first in the new nest. The nest was too high off the ground for us to reach and the leaf too heavy for her to lift. We thought she might build a new nest somewhere else. Within a couple of hours, the tiny bird had begun construction of the second floor, on top of the leaf. It was a thing of beauty when she finished, and six weeks later she fledged two chicks.

Bomb's Away

I was out in the backyard dreaming up some silly idea one morning and noticed a pair of ravens flying by. One of the birds had a rather large branch in its mouth. As they flew over a leafless pecan tree next door, the bird with the stick let go of it. I watched it fall. It twirled straight down over the top of a perched red-tailed hawk, scoring a direct hit. The hawk let out a loud squawk, jumped off the limb and quickly flew away. I didn't know ravens could do that, did you?

The Crossing

I saw a note on the kitchen table that said come to the river at 8:00 AM. I forgot about breakfast and headed out. Our new friend, with her rescued Polish Arabian horse, was going to the river for a second attempt to make a crossing. My friend was a trainer, and had been working with the horse for a year and a half to reach this very important moment.

This side of the river is a small strip of land, great to ride or hike. But across the water the trail led off into the wilderness with miles and miles of surprise and wonder.

The rescued horse had spent twelve years locked up in an 8 foot by 12 foot pen. He had no idea what the world was really like and I didn't want to miss this moment.

I arrived just as the girls were heading down to the water. I don't wear shoes much so I passed around the horse and wadded out to the middle of the creek to show him how deep the water was.

The beautiful white Polish Arabian horse (looking very much like a unicorn) circled a few times and finally stepped on the edge of the water. Then taking off the lead rope, our rider climbed on. The horse was hesitating for a moment, but my friend moved in behind him waving a stick (sometimes we all need a little push from behind). It was easier to move forward towards me than to retreat, so here the horse came. I stepped out of the way, and our brave horse climbed the far bank of the river and stood relishing the moment. His head was up and proud of his great accomplishment. Then he turned and started up the calling dusty road of the unknown. It was a beautiful moment. He was snorting with every step he took .

They were gone for two hours. When we saw them again, he was a completely different horse.

The Roar of the Dinosaurs

I love peace and quiet, and it's hard to find nowadays. The only time I ever get some is walking in the middle of the night.

There's a perfect time to go walking around here, which is about 3:00 AM. That's when those who stay up late, go to bed, and it's before the early birds start to stir. On this day, I get up and have some oatmeal, drink some coffee and drive over to a local trail head. I put on a jacket, take off my shoes, grab a nice walking stick and head up a big hill into the peaceful darkness. I have found it's a good idea to tap my stick every once in a while so the beasts of the night know I am out and about.

I was enjoying the wonderful quiet when it was interrupted by a big, loud pickup truck somewhere off in the night. Someone young and wild trying to impress the ladies, I thought. Then as that noise faded away, a huge,flashing 300-seat flying movie theater came blowing over with the roar of the engines following along about a mile behind.

"Where did all this roaring noise come from anyway?"

My mind shifted into a place that I can only get to alone. It said, "It's the roar of the dinosaurs." A billion barrels of dragon fat stored underground for millions of years sucked up by giant rocker pumps. Then it's boiled to purify the flammable part so it will fit thru small stainless steel pipes.Then it's squirted into strange places where it gets squeezed and lit on fire, where it comes roaring out as some odd thing called horsepower. It pushes or pulls these obnoxious machines up and down roads, out into the skys or across oceans making more noise than anybody can stand.

I went and helped dig up these old dragon's bones years ago, and realized the chickens were a lot bigger than they are now. That's why there's so much of this dragon grease everywhere. As I stop and ponder this revelation in the moonlight, I realize the dinosaurs are not gone. Their belly fat is still dripping out everywhere, and they are one of the reasons why the place is so noisy.

I walked off up the trail and sat down on my favorite rock to enjoy the wonderful little town I live in . Then off in the distance I heard a new sound, a rooster crowing in the dark. I am reminded of the fact that they are related to the Tyrannosaurus rex. Then I try to imagine what a big male rex sounded like when he rared back and roared in the middle of the night. It's no wonder even their oil is noisy. The dinosaurs are still with us, aren't they?

A Rising

This morning I was out for a quiet pre-dawn walk to count shooting stars (there were two) when I noticed a strange point of light behind the far hills. It got taller, brighter and began to curve, slowly turning into a lovely sliver of the moonrise.

Monday

It's Monday and it's been a week since the new bear came into my life. He's a big black male, maybe 400lbs. I've had to change my pre-dawn walk habits to suit his presence. I've decided to call him Monday since it's trash day and that's the day we met.

For five days in a row he has been roughing up the trash cans around here. I show up and he takes off down the dirt road at a full gallop. When those big flat feet of his hit the ground, it sounds like a horse wearing shower shoes. The last two nights my new friend hasn't been around, but I still listen intently for any possible noise he might make.

It's 3:56 AM, and the harvest moon will be full in four minutes. As I ease carefully along, I begin to hear a new sound in the distance. It sounds like a pack of coyotes calling each other in the moonlight, so I stop and listen. The sounds are getting louder. It worries me as they seem to be coming closer. The moon is off to the west and the sounds are coming from the east.

As they get closer and the sounds get clearer, I realize there is a huge flock of geese coming towards me. As they pass over me, I can finally see them and I am overwhelmed with joy. 'Wild Geese That Fly With The Moon On Their Wings'…and I must admit they are one of my favorite things. Their shadows block the moonlight at the exact moment the moon turns full, and I am so grateful to have been there.

The Newspaper Man

It's 5:30AM and the sun won't be up for an hour and a half. I'm out for an early walk to enjoy the peace and quiet. I see something big and black shooting down the road towards me. In the low light it looks like a small bear, but as it gets a little closer it turns into three skunks running in tight formation with their tails sticking straight up (this is even more disturbing then the bear). I step off the road to give them the right of way. They see me and prance across the road to climb a large boulder and watch me as I ease on by. It's a mother with two nearly grown young stinkers, livening up my morning.

I start moving again towards the top of the hill to maybe catch the sunrise. It's very quiet. Between the early bird songs, I hear an unnatural sound. A poorly tuned old engine laboring through our little town. It's running up and down the streets, speeding up way too fast and slowing down as well. Everytime it slows down, the brakes screech. The radio is on full blast to some god awful talk show.

Oh no, now he's coming up the road I'm on! His headlights are on high beams! I can hear the newspapers flying out the windows, flopping on the driveways of his clients. The latest news is being delivered to their doorstep. I'm turning down a dirt road as he catches up with me.

I'm feeling very annoyed by all the disruption of my peaceful morning walk. He turns around right where I'm standing, covering me with noise, dust and car exhaust. While I stand there looking at him with disgust in his messy old worn out car, he leans out the window and says "Good Morning" in the sweetest tone. I am immediately transformed into a great appreciator of our wonderful newspaper delivery man. Kindness is magic.

Thank God for Horses

Now from what I've been led to believe, horses have been hauling us and our belongings around for a long time. For thousands of years, the equine members of planet earth have been very important forms of transportation to human beings. However, lately things have changed. We have developed all kinds of technology and machines to do the dirty work of everyday life. Our horses have been placed on the back burner (so to speak). But I'm not so sure you appreciate how lucky we men are to still have them around.

We were gifted an Andalusian horse named Apollo that I just love, so I have been hanging around the ranch enjoying my new friend lately. He is the same kind of horse Napoleon Bonaparte rode.

A lot of times when I get done playing with Apollo, I sit and watch what goes on. If you are quiet, no one even knows you're there. It's mostly women that love horses, and it's frightening to see what goes on out there in the evening. They are mothering those poor horses something awful: sticking fly masks on their heads, squirtin' them with stinky essential oils, painting on cortisone, spraying them with bug off, wrapping their legs with padded booties and fly socks, giving them garlic powder to make them taste bad to the flys, washing them down with flowery shampoos, braiding their manes and tails, polishing their hooves after picking their feet with some kind of hook tool, and the list goes on. Then they get on and ride them around in circles makin' them do strange things, "Gitty up, Wooooo, Stand, Back, Back, Back." It's a wonder the horses put up with it all.

Then I got to thinking, what would it be like if we didn't have horses for the women to put all that hovering and motherly love into? That really scared me because they would be doing all that stuff to us. Polishing our toenails and braiding our hair, wiping us down with three or four different smelly creams, squirting us with fly spray, rubbing us with liniment and telling us "Back, Back, Back."

I sat there thinking about it for a few minutes and said quietly to myself, "Thank God for Horses."

The Kanuck

I met ol' Ralph at 'The Donut Hole' (a coffee shop in Meiners Oaks) many years ago. He was in his mid eighties. As a merchant seaman, he had spent his life on the ocean. He was a 'Kanuck' from the west coast of Canada. He heard that we were making a totem pole and wanted to come see it.

Ralph had lots of old friends that were west coast Indians, and spoke several native languages. He had known Bill Reed, Willie Seaweed and a few other totem pole carving greats over the years. He spent many hot afternoons sitting around our shop behind the Estill's family estate telling wonderful stories about his long and colorful life. Ralph had hauled freight from Alaska to Vancouver and all places in between, even working at times for the Queen. But my favorite story of his had nothing to do with totem poles or the queen.

We were having a barbecue out back in Hughie's yard one evening talking boats and fishing when Ralph stopped by. He sat and listened to it all for a long time. Ralph got real quiet and serious, then he said. "It was a dark moonless night just after the beginning of the second world war. I joined the Canadian coast guard. They didn't have any gun boats in service that early in the war, so we put to sea in a small fishing boat they used for patrolling coastal waters at night. All our lights were shut down and we were running in a blackout. Our job was to stop any boats we found and come aboard to check their paperwork. Then he paused and said, "We just had military rifles for armament."

They were somewhere down near Orcas Island slowly patrolling the Strait of Juan de Fuca when out of the fog came a huge warship at full speed. Ralph's captain swung the small fishing boat around and cut into the huge ship's path. They turned on their small spot light to stop the ship for an inspection and check the paperwork. The massive ship just kept right on coming at full speed. Ralph's little boat had to swerve out of the way at the last possible moment to keep from being hit broadside. The wake from the huge passing ship washed over them like a breaking wave. Then right behind that first ship came the whole United States Pacific Fleet: destroyers, cruisers, battleships and carriers, followed by support craft and submarines.

Ralph's Coastguard fishing boat was swerving back and forth in the huge wakes as the gigantic vessels sped by at full steam ahead. The ocean turned into a washing machine as the monstrous boat wakes met each other. Ralph said," It was the worst seas I had ever seen, all caused by passing ships in the total darkness of night. The Pacific fleet was moving as fast as they could to avoid possible Japanese torpedoes, some going forty knots." Ralph continued, "But it was the most amazing night of my entire life, no one even noticed we were there. By the time we got back to the harbor we realized what had just happened and decided not to tell anyone, just for the safety of the American fleet."

Well after a story like that, we all decided he was the winner of the boat story telling contest hands down.

Pretty Cold Winter

The Indian summer in Alaska and the storms of fall were late. A call came in for a delivery of a nice prefab cedar log home. It looked like there was a small window in the weather to make the trip happen. We loaded the log home up for the twelve hour boat ride across Cook Inlet. It was going to an Alieut man in a village on the Alaska peninsula. He asked if we could set it up for him, but no one wanted to work that far away this late in the fall, and the boat had to be dry docked for the winter. The captain told him he would come back first thing in the spring, with a crew and set it up for him then. The sea was stormy all the way back to Homer and just a miserable trip, I was glad to fly south a few days later.

The next spring when I returned, the boat was headed back across the inlet to assemble the beautiful log home and I tagged along. When we arrived at the beach where we left the bundled sections of the house, it was gone. The captain said, "We're here to put your house up, where is it?" The old alieut smiled and said,

"Hey, pretty cold winter can you get me another one?"

We Too

It's early up here on the mountain the first day of March, and I am finishing a morning walk. Suddenly, piercing through the silence, I hear what sounds very much like a rivet hammer. I stop, climb a small rise and ease around the side of a hill to get a better look at where the sound is coming from. To my suprise, I found a red shafted Flicker (a type of woodpecker) sitting on the top of the closed door of the observatory dome. He is calling, "We too, We too, We too". Then he stops ,takes a look around and brings his beak down to the metal roof. With a sudden burst of movement, he unloads a jolt of fifty or so pecks into the turret of the telescope. The sound is a surprisingly loud burst that can be heard for a mile in all directions. Then he switches back to his "We too We too We too" call.

As I stand there watching, he flies over to the cap on the top of the sewer vent, gives it a few "We toos" and unloads a jolt of pecks on it. It is smaller and has a much higher pitched sound than the dome, and it can be heard for a considerable distance as well. He pecks the cap several times (he seems to like the tone). Then he glides over to the weather station nearby. He gets a good grip on it, braces with his tail, calls out three more, "We toos" and hammers the weather station .

He then swoops over to a walnut tree and resumes his pecking and singing once again. As I turn to leave, I notice a lovely female flicker has landed nearby and appears to be very impressed with his wonderful display of percussionary skill.

Who?

You know, from all the stories I write about hiking up some trail, it sounds like that's all I do. I actually work all the time making beautiful, thought provoking things but that is not as fun to talk about. Making things is not as interesting as where the ideas come from. Most of my ideas come along when I get away from the outside influence of other people, and let my imagination soar.

That's what I was doing this very morning when I heard the owls. There are two of them. One has a low hoot and the other has a high one. I hear them in a sycamore tree near where I have walked for many years, early in the dawning light of morning. They see me coming and start asking, "Who, Who, Who?"

For some reason I think, "Who? Who do you think? It's me, the barefooted guy with the walking stick and the long white hair. Do you birds have a short term memory problem? I'm here every day!"

The birds just keep on asking, "Who, Who, Who," but I'm no longer sure I give a hoot!

Bicycle Bubble Machines

I have always enjoyed inventing joyful things to make myself happy. Over the years I have had the privilege of working with several very bright people. John Dee Cuccio introduced me to bubble toys, he had some successful inventions with patents, mostly in the field of bubbles. The bubble inside the bubble and the swing around Bubble Bee sold very well. (I worked on the bubble brush with him). He got me thinking about and making new ideas.

John helped finance some of the parts for parade floats I later built, like 'Old Hoover The Monster Of Lake Casitas.' When I was working on the second fish, I decided to put a frog on a bicycle for the fish to chase down the street. The fish had bubbles coming out of the gills so it seemed like a good idea to give the frog some bubbles too! A wind powered bubble machine seemed feasible, so after a trip to the scrap yard and the thrift store, I built myself a prototype. I put it on the back of my bike but it didn't work because my body was blocking the wind. I had Jimmy Robertson build a little metal jib that stuck out off to the side behind the seat to hook the machine on. When I took off down the street for the first test ride, it sprang to life, producing a massive trail of bubbles. I was looking back at the bubble maker working better than I ever dreamed, when I promptly ran into the back of a parked car. I got up feeling stupid and took off again in thinking this thing was pretty cool. I peddled into a housing tract, with less constricted space, looking like a small weather system coming down the street in a cloud of bubbles.

I began to think about what to buy with all the money I was going to make when suddenly my dream was interrupted. To my shock and surprise, a small gang of wild eyed junior high school boys on bicycles appeared seemingly from out of nowhere. They chased me up the street screaming and yelling, swerving through my wonderful wall of bubbles in a popping frenzy. All at once, the two leaders locked handle bars and crashed in the street directly in front of all the other crazed cyclists. There was a huge collision and all the rest of the bicycles were tangled and wound up in a heap in the middle of the street. As I looked back to see no one was seriously hurt, my thoughts of huge never-ending wealth ran out with the bubble soap. I could see there might be problems with this idea as a toy, so I just kept right on peddling back to the garage and closed the door.

P.S. The bicycle bubble machine worked great in the parades though.

Just a Thought

I was out for a walk this morning and I noticed the wild oats were once again hanging over the trail. Having suffered an attack from a small tick recently, I had my eye out for places they might be hanging out (because they don't need to hide). Sure enough, as I studied the thin stem farthest out in the trail, I spotted a tick! I should have better things to do than watch bugs, but I got to thinking. How did this tiny little insect about the size of a tomato seed have the vision and insight to find this trail? That in itself was amazing. Then from her viewpoint crawling around on the ground, (less than an 1/8 of an inch tall), selected and climbed the right wild oat stalk, to put herself in a perfect spot to catch a hair on my leg. If the tick were, say, as big as I am, the oat stem would be two hundred feet tall and there would be literally millions of them to choose from just in this area alone. It would take some great eyes to select the right one to climb to end up out in the middle of the trail, and by the way how did she know this was the trail ? Or better yet, how would she know what a trail even was? It would seem to me that these bugs are a lot smarter than I ever gave them credit for, capable of some real Intelligence, reasoning, and problem solving skills.

They are fearless little hunters and we are their prey. It would be like me climbing a tall tree on the side of a canyon sized pathway, and grabbing on to a three hundred foot tall beast passing by and digging a hole in it's skin and dining. Then I would swell up forty times my original size, drop to the ground and lay my thirty thousand eggs, probably under some rock, to hatch next year.

I picked the tick off the oat stem and admired her for a long moment, said a little prayer for her, laid her on a rock and smashed her flat! Then I got to thinking, there must be a tiny tick school somewhere maybe under that same rock. It has little chairs and a green chalkboard on the wall. The teacher takes a stick and points to a picture on the wall of me, kind of like they have at the acupuncturist office, and shows the baby ticks what I look like and the best points to bite. Then she explains what a trail is and which oat stem is best to climb to catch me. They have a little graduation, throw their hats in the air, give each other big hugs, and it's off to catch a big Dennis. In the fall when all of them get back together, they must have amazing stories to tell!

Native American Music

I was out snooping around the desert southwest one spring, and I found myself driving by the Papago Indian Reservation. I decided to swing in and take a look. There were a couple of rows of clapboard houses, probably built by the government many years ago, surrounded by old cars up on blocks. It was too hot to grow anything but cactus. There were lines of rocks around where the grass should have been. I idled along checking the place out. About half way down the street it looked like there might be something going on, a party maybe. There were several cars parked around this one place. Out on a covered patio in front of the house sat a bunch of tough looking Indians. They gave the eye as I went by. I just kept going but I noticed there was a band playing and they were playing the blues. I had spent about ten years in good bands singing and playing harmonica and I could really play. On my way back down the street I pulled over in front of the party house, got out and walked up to those tough looking Indians. I said, "Hey you guys sound pretty good, can I sit in?"

They didn't know what to say, they just looked at me for a minute and then one of them said, "What do you play white boy?" I pulled out a D harmonica and gave them a snappy little riff.

The guitar player said, "Grab the other microphone," as he started into the song 'If the River was Whiskey and I was a Divin' Duck.' I spent the rest of the afternoon on that porch playing Indian music, and I left about dark with a bunch of new friends.

Roadrunner

I was visiting an old friend one day, a while back, and asked how things were going. "Great" he said, "I've been adopted by a pair of roadrunners". He took me outside and showed me a rough stick nest stuck in a tree crotch about ten feet from his back door. We walked over and looked at the two chicks sitting in a moss filled nest in an almond tree.

"They've been here about a month;" he said, "they like the food I put out for the abandoned cats. People bring their house cats out here and dump them, so I have to feed them. The birds just moved in and built a nest near the cat food."

At the time, I was waiting for a new engine for my VW van to arrive in a few days, so it was a nice opportunity to watch the roadrunners up close and personal. The birds were great providers with a steady flow of lizards, bugs, mice, birds and snakes. Everything was dead when they brought it home, but some of the meals were pretty big. Often during meals, the snakes were half swallowed and half sticking out while the roadrunners were eating. It was sort of a gas gauge, when the snake was finally swallowed it was time for more food. In between big meals, the chicks got cat food or frogs.

The adult roadrunners only flew from the nest to the ground. They walked up the tree trunk and when they hit the ground leaving they were running (thus the name I suppose). They didn't hunt together, one went one way and the other went another. As they moved around, much like coyotes, they made a little sound to let each other know where they were. It was a high pitched call that got lower and lower in pitch, much like a sad puppy whimpering. They also had a soft throat chortel and sometimes clucked like a chicken. I got on to their different calls and would mimic them. They didn't much like my sad puppy call or the clucking, but when I got close and chortled, they would stop and want to play.

I found one out in a pasture one early morning, and gave it a tongue rattle (chortle). The bird flew down the fence line going in and out of the posts in a playful little flirt, landing out in the middle of the horse arena and chortled back. Flexing her tail feathers up and down several times, she did a little dance and raised her lovely hood. I don't know what it all meant, but I felt honored with her response. They are such brilliant birds!

One day while I was putting the new engine in my van I heard the chirp of a red-shouldered hawk, a notorious bird hunter. I crawled out from under my bus to see what was going to happen. I thought, oh those poor roadrunners must be in trouble. The hawk came in and landed on a high limb in the nesting tree. All of a sudden the roadrunner jumped out of the nest, flew and ran up the tree diving headlong into the surprised bird of prey. So many feathers were flying it was hard to tell what was going on. When I finally could see, the roadrunner had one foot on a branch and the other holding a leg of the hawk, yanking large mouthfuls of plumage out. The red-shouldered hawk was doing everything it could think of to get loose. It was snowing feathers when it finally broke free. It flew off, hotly pursued by a very angry squawking roadrunner.

After seeing that performance I fell hopelessly in love with roadrunners.

Whale Rider

One cold foggy morning in Alaska, I looked out and saw humpback whales moving around in Tutka Bay. I ran over and got a kayak down and paddled out to watch them go by. Having absolutely no experience with whales in the ocean, I was a babe in the waves. There was a little breeze on the water when I got out of the lagoon. The whales were headed my way so I sat and waited for them to resurface; they were down for a long time. Then I noticed a big circle of air bubbles coming up and anchovies jumping everywhere. Suddenly huge black open jaws of whales burst from the sea all around me, as big as school buses, sticking 15 feet out of the water. Fish were flying everywhere! Finally the last whale to come up bumped my kayak and nearly knocked me into the swerling melee. It was too bad I was so scared because they were so close I could have climbed on. The whale's breath smelled like hot fish soup. When I got back to the beach there were thirteen anchovies in my kayak and I had them for lunch. From then on, when I saw whales coming I watched them from the beach!

Where There's Frogs

I was making a tree frog sitting on a leaf at the Cayucos sand sculpture contest on the 4th of July one year. A wonderful mystical older woman hobbled up and stopped to watch. She looked as though she might be a witch. She stood there for a moment lost in her thoughts, then she spoke,"I just love frogs. Where there's frogs, there's water and where there's water, there's food. And where there's food there's peace." Then she reached into her shiny little hand-beaded bag, grabbed a pinch of green glitter and threw it on my frog. She smiled at me, turned and slowly disappeared into the early morning mist.

Air Out

My friend Mary, a soft gentle soul, is the mother of many wonderful children. She was out talking to me in my shop, under the big oak tree, many years ago. She told me her kids cracked her up. Mary had some great stories, but one story that I remember was hilarious.

"I was changing my youngest child," she said, "while one of my sons sat and watched." She took off the diaper and layed the child on a small table by the bed.

The little boy said, "Why did you lay her there?"

Mary said, "I'm letting her air out."

The shocked little boy looked up and said, "Letting her air out!?!"

A Coyote Tail

The unusually warm snap in the middle of winter in Ojai had turned cold once again. Coming down a steep trail early in the morning, I noticed some movement ahead of me. It was a coyote focusing on something in the grass. It looked like it might be a snake. The coyote was harassing the snake, nipping at it several times. The snake was cold and sluggish, unable to defend itself well. As I got closer I could see it was a large rattlesnake.

Suddenly the coyote lunged like lightning, grabbing the snake's tail. He whipped the snake over his head and slapped it back and forth, smacking it on the ground about five or six times. It was so fast that I could hardly believe it. The snake was knocked senseless. Then the coyote bit the snake in two and walked off with the tail. The coyote went over and laid down under a tree and ate his breakfast. Then while I watched, the coyote came back over and bit the head off the snack and happily lopped off with a little something for the kids. Later on I found the bitten off rattle of the snake.

I sat down and tried to imagine myself grabbing a big rattlesnake by the tail with my teeth and slapping it senselessly on the ground in the name of breakfast. That would take some real confidence, skill, and foolhardy courage! That coyote was fearless and what an athlete.

To this day I am still amazed at what I saw. I'm glad I'm not that brave…

Calamari

Ed Bernie and I drove down from Cambria to take a look at the three giant smokestacks in Morro bay. They had been decommissioned as a power plant recently. The bid to take them down was millions of dollars, and we were hoping to come up with some artistic creative new use for them.

We drove down and parked near the main gate and got out for a better look. The oil-powered steam electric-generation plant wasn't very impressive from a distance, but when we got up close, it was humongous.

Before we even got started, I was surprised by all the wildlife that had moved into the abandoned grounds. There was a herd of deer grazing on native grass that sprinted off as we approached. Every tree seemed to have an overstuffed blue heron's nest in it . Hundreds of seagulls stood around keeping an eye on us, along with many other beach birds.

Everything else was forgotten as we tilted our heads back to look up at the towering smoke stacks. They were so tall, they felt like the exhaust smoke of three space shuttles taking off at the same time that had turned into cement. They were fifty feet across at ground level, rising nearly seven hundred feet tall. There were tiny little step ladders going up the outside of each one that felt like the stairway to heaven. Whoever had to climb them was probably glad he lost his job.I could just hear the boss telling him, "Okay Louie, climb up there and see if the chimney is clean." The stacks were apparently designed to put the smoke in the stratosphere. They were so tall the birds wouldn't even sit on them.

My friend Ed was thinking about making the smokestacks into an observation tower. He was a retired 'contractor of the year ' from Orange County. Ed told us, "If you put toilets up there, the pressure from the water falling that far would blow the pipes out." We were both overwhelmed with the immensity of the project so we decided to have some fish soup at a local restaurant and forget about it.

We got a window seat down by the bay, ordered some fish soup and sat watching the tide going out, waiting for our food. A seagull flew up and landed on a cement shelf next to a stone wall that was being slowly exposed by the falling tide near our window. The bird ignored us and stared at something on the wall, and we started watching him. He walked back and forth several times looking intently at something, then he walked over, stood on his tip toes and grabbed a tiny little brown thing and started pulling. It stretched out like a lumpy rubber band. The gull put his feet up on the wall so he could use his whole strength and body weight to pull it up. The rubber band thing kept getting longer and longer. Suddenly the seagull fell flat on his back, as the young octopus popped loose from his crack in the wall and completely covered the gulls head. The bird flapped his head around trying to get the octopus off his face and must have lost his grip. In one lovely little flip the octopus landed in the ocean in a cloud of black ink and quickly disappeared.

Just about then, the waiter brought us our lunch. The soup was fish, clams, mussels and calamari with carrots and potatoes. Our octopus didn't get away.

Find a Need and Fill It

I wrote this story to tell at a costume party. The story is about people from the gold rush of California. And the story really happened.

I was up where the angels camp, during the gold rush. The rent was due. I sat on the porch of the boarding house where I was living, worried about paying my rent. Waking from my thoughts I noticed a miner standing in the street eyeing me. I said, "Howdy ,what can I do for you?"

He walked over close to where I was sitting, looked both ways to make sure no one was listening and in a low voice he said, "You look big and strong, can I trust you?"

"Well I hope so, what do you need?" I said.

"I need help carrying something really heavy, I will give you $10 and buy you dinner."

"Well what's the story," I asked?

The gentleman explained it all, "I was out prospecting this morning and saw something shiny in the water. I waded out in the creek, pushed the gravel back and that shine just kept getting bigger and bigger. It was such a huge chunk of gold I couldn't pick it up, so I covered it back up and came to town to find someone to help me carry it. Will you give me a hand?"

I thought about it for a moment and said, "This whole thing sounds dangerous to me, a fella could get killed carrying that much gold around. Ten bucks and dinner ain't enough to die for, if you want my help you got to give me half." The miner got all red in the face, turned and stomped off.

I was still sitting on the porch worrying about the rent when he came easing back over. He stood there for a long moment and finally said, "Ok damn it, but we better hurry up before someone else finds it."

We stopped and got a piece of canvas to wrap around it. On our way down the creek, I found a strong limb to use as a handle so we could both lift. The gold was still there and when we dug it out of the gravel, it was nearly too big for the two of us to carry. We wrapped it in canvas and tied a big knot, stuck the limb through and struggled to pick it up. With the help of greed and fear, we managed to stagger up the creek and back to angels camp. I was afraid someone would ask us what we were carrying, but no one did. I'm sure it looked so heavy nobody wanted to get involved.

When we got to the assayers office and unwrapped the huge nugget they couldn't believe their eyes. They didn't have a scale big enough to weigh it. We had to take it down to the livery stable to get a number. It was the biggest gold nugget ever found. One hundred ninety-eight pounds and change.

Now I'm rich and I can buy anything I want. When people ask what they can do to get rich like me, I just tell them...just find a need and fill it!

The River of Gold

It's not really a river, just a seasonal creek. Most of the time the water doesn't even make it to the ocean. Every once in a while, if it rains enough, the water will swell up and flow across the built up sand bar opening it to the sea. That's when the steelhead trout swim in to lay their eggs. This also changes the behavior of the tourists. The tourists usually get here early for their appointed bus ride up into the national monument. While they are waiting they see the lovely beach down below and decide to take a quick morning walk. They are usually all dressed up in fancy clothes wearing their best jewelry and expensive shoes. When they come down to the beach and run into the small stream flowing across the sand, they stop. It's too much trouble to bend down and take their shoes off so they get back and take a little run at it. They launch themselves across the flowing water. Invariably when they come down, things not designed for hard landings come off. Bracelets, necklaces, rings and earware go flying.

The funny thing about gold is when it gets warm from being worn, you hardly notice when it comes loose and lands in the water. Later in the day when I come walking, I am always amazed at the lovely assortment of jewelry I find in the river of gold.

The Mattress Man

Out walking one morning in the May gray when I was caught and passed by a very enthusiastic young man. He said good morning and headed on carrying a couple of upholstered foam rubber pads and a bag of chalk, wearing some very fancy climbing shoes that caught my eye. He disappeared down a side canyon off the main trail and I walked on and forgot all about him. On my way back down the hill I stopped and was watching some bird's build a nest in a small hole in a sugar maple limb. Suddenly there was a loud… AAAAAAAAAAAAHH….yell.! It was coming from the same canyon where I saw the mattress man go. I stood there for a moment wondering what to do,and decided to go and see what had happened, to make sure he wasn't hurt. As I got closer I heard him scream again, this time with some unprintable adjectives and adverbs. Finally I could see him. He was lying in a pile on his mattresses under a large overhanging rock,down near the creek. There were white chalk marks leading up the rock to a place where they stopped, an overhang about halfway to the top.

As I sat and watched, he tried climbing again. Chalking up, he carefully gripped the huge stone, finding little places to hold on with his fingers and fancy shoes. He worked his way up to the pitiless outcropping and once again slipped and fell into a heap on his matress.The terrible noise that erupted from the mattress man shocked my tender ears in this wonderfully quiet place in the woods. But I was glad to see I wouldn't be carrying him back to civilization. I sat and watched him try two more times and wanted to offer some helpful advice: take the foam pads away and your climbing will improve! But instead I just turned and walked away.

The Shape Shifter

I was out walking over the Ojai browse way early one morning, when I happened upon my artist friend Shahastra, perched upon a rock beside the trail. Somewhere in our conversation she mentioned that she had been reading about the early Native Americans. The book said that certain tribes had special individuals, (medicine men and women) who had mastered the art of shapeshifting. She asked me if I knew anything about the subject. I stood and thought about it for a moment and said, "Yes, I've had first hand experience with shape shifting." I began to tell her my tale.

Wandering in the Arizona desert years ago coming down a game trail, I noticed fresh hoof prints ahead. I saw just a few at first that I thought might be from a young deer. But as I continued the whole trail became covered with these tiny hoof marks. Rounding a curve in the path, I happen upon a small desert pig with her head stuck in a bush, hiding. The rest of her was sticking out in the sunshine. It dawned on me that I had been following a quite large 'root' of peccary, feeding among the cactus.

I stopped in my tracks as the pigs, (maybe sixty of them) began to clack their three-inch tusks. They were all around me. When wild peccary feel threatened they all snap their mouths open and closed in a curiously alarming little rhythm. They are not very big but they all charge at the same time. I realized that I was in big trouble. Not being able to fly, I looked around for a safe place and noticed all the trees were covered with thorns, which are no fun to climb. I slowly backed away and found myself shape shifted. I was magically transformed from a fearless desert explorer into a great big chicken. Lucky for me, I got away.

Thermals

When the temperature is down in the forties at night, I notice that the trail is cold on my feet in the morning. As I pick my way softly along, I feel a warm place up under the oak trees. The sun isn't up yet, so I stop and stand for a moment. It feels warmer here. I walk back down the trail and the ground gets cold again. I don't believe my feet so I go back to the warm spot and stand. This spot is warmer! I still don't believe it. I walk off doubting my senses.

The next day, I hadn't forgotten about the warm spot so I stopped and felt the ground again in the same spot. It's warm! There is no reason for It to be warm, but it's warm. The sun won't be up for twenty minutes; I walk on and the trail gets cold again.

The next morning I decided to climb the nearby creek for a change of pace. I can smell a whiff of sulfur. There is water coming from cracks in the rock on the creek. The water is flowing off to the side of the main stream and it looks cloudy and gray. I stick my foot in it. It's cold. I'm still a ways below the warm spot on the trail. I keep climbing. I begin to see orange algae in the water off to the side of the main flow. I'm not sure, but the water seems warmer on my feet. I don't believe it so I stick my feet in both streams at the same time. One is warm and the other is cold. I'm thrilled as I continue upstream. Then I see the source of the warm water coming out from under a tree root. I stick my size 12 foot into the small pool. It's even warmer than the last place I stepped.

My bare feet have found this wonderful discovery for me. When you get used to barefoot walking, it's like walking on your hands. My feet tell me so much, I'm always amazed! When I put shoes on, I miss half the walk.

I'm not going to tell you shoe lovers where my warm spring is. Take your shoes off and go for a walk. Maybe you will find where the trail is warm too!

Polynya

I always thought polynya would be a great name for a restaurant in Alaska. A polynya is the first place where the ice melts in the spring and they are always crowded with life. Early hunters were drawn to them by the sound. The north is so quiet in winter and large gatherings of birds and sea mammals make a lot of noise. That meant abundant food for hungry hunters.

There was a polynya up in Homer where all the fishermen congregated early in the morning. At 5:00 AM it was the place to be. The cooks would be flipping sausage and eggs, the waitress was taking orders and pouring hot coffee. The stories would be flying. It was one of the few places in the world where you didn't want to be late. Just finding out what happened yesterday was worth the cold bumpy boat ride across the bay. Wild amazing things were quite normal in Alaska, and to hear them told firsthand by the men and women who were there was sensational. Just about anywhere you go, there are morning polynya's with great people, full of wit, wisdom and humor. They tell true stories that surprise and entertain.

Cambria's coffee den is one of those places. There is a core group of locals that open conversations and invite others to join in. A good cup of strong coffee and the lips go to flapping, and there you are…talking big.

One morning, the good old boys were gathered round telling stories about building fantasyland for Disney, or how they ran a clothing company like Two Potato (they made the Hawaiian shirts), when a new guy came moseying up looking for some coffee. The boys checked him out and invited him to sit and join in like they did most everyone. He just looked interesting and when someone asked him what he had done for a living, he sheepishly said he taught Astrophysics for a big college in Los Angeles. He had worked for NASA on the moon landing too. (He was one of those people who could project the course for a landing on Mars, and actually hit it). He taught physics for twenty-five years at UC Irvine. He was a great guy named Eugene. He was retired and lived in a nice house up in the Lamerts part of town.

Ed Bernie, the contractor that built Fantasyland, invited him to go for a walk with us later that morning, in the bullpen above San Simeon. Eugene was not an outdoors kind of guy but he showed up.He was a little nervous when we ducked under the fence to the bullpen because there were bulls in sight. He was worried about me going barefoot. I told him I would be ok. He admitted he had never been out in the country before, and was amazed how beautiful it was. His whole life had been spent studying the stars and mathematics. We worked our way around the bulls and climbed up the hill to the magic forest, where giant oak trees have all grown sideways because of the constant wind from the sea. The trees are all lying down,12 feet tall, 60 feet long and hundreds of years old. Eugene was dazzled, but the highlight of our walk was down in the ancient Native American midden piles near the beach. In the sand dunes Eugene kneeled down and found his first flint arrowhead! He nearly fainted.

Inner Tube Fishing

Back before I realized how little I knew, I would sit on the beach and watch people fish in the kelp beds off of Mondo's cove. It seemed like every time I looked out there I would see someone pulling a fish into their boat. I like to eat fish but they cost too much. I got to thinking, I don't have a boat but if I got me an intertube, I could paddle out there with my trout pole and catch some nice fish.

A couple of days later I was back with a patched old inner tube and my fishing pole with a bag of mackerel for bait. I also brought a straw hat for shade and a short piece of cotton rope to tie my catch on, and pushed myself out past the surf line. With my pole across my lap, I paddled out to the kelp beds. I remember intentionally leaving my pocket knife behind for fear of rust.

I baited my hook and let out some line. In no time at all, I caught two nice rock bass and tied them to the cotton rope that I had tied to the belt loop on my pants. I was putting on some more bait when I felt a pretty good tug on my pants loop. I dropped the baited hook in the water, and reached down and grabbed my fish rope. Something had taken my fish, all I had left was a shorter piece of rope. As I sat there wondering what had just happened, I felt a swish of water on my leg and the fish line started going out, so I grabbed my pole. When I locked the reel, my pole bent and the innertube started to move. Slowly at first and when I set the hook, me and my patched up old tube really took off. Now I was kicking up quite a wake, heading out to sea at an alarming rate. It was about then that I realized I was the one that was caught. Remembering that I left my knife on shore, and too cheap to let go of the fishing pole, I released the drag on my reel and immediately came to a halt. I sat and watched the spool of line get smaller and smaller. Finally the last wrap went up the pole and disappeared into the ocean.I had gotten away.

It was a long paddle back to shore and when I stepped up on the beach, I had a much better understanding of how it felt to be a fish.

Rick's Rocket

Rick was a mechanical wizard, and because everything he worked on (he worked on airplanes) had to be perfect, otherwise someone might die. Because of the stress he was the biggest grump ever. My old friend Hughie used to say, "He's not mad, he's just got experience."

Rick's favorite pastime was wandering around the local scrap metal yards, looking for weird things people had thrown away. When I stopped by, he would always take me out and show me his latest discoveries. This time it was a nice tricycle with cast aluminum spoke wheels and a small jet engine, used to power the electrical generation systems on an outdated passenger plane. It was so small I could hardly believe it was a jet engine. It looked like a vacuum cleaner with lots of small stainless tubing running around on it. The metal tag on the side of it said it was made by general electric, and among other things it had 60 pounds of thrust. It was cute but I didn't think much about it at the time.

The next time I stopped by Rick, he had the jet engine bolted to the tricycle with a small fuel tank plumbed in under a new well-padded motorcycle seat. There was a helmet and safety goggles wrapped around the handle bars. The petals had been replaced by two substantial foot pegs. There also appeared to be a small disc brake on the back axle, controlled by a lever on the handle bars. The bike frame had a new coat of red paint with flame decals.

Rick had a new scuff on his cheek and right arm. I was standing there looking it all over when he asked me if I wanted to take it for a little spin. To avoid saying no, I asked him where he got the road rash. He looked at me sheepishly and said on his third pass across the field, he hit a little bump and left the planet for a few seconds. On re-entry he wasn't going straight when he hit the ground, and did a little endo.

"It's safe if you keep it under 50 MPH, but look out when you start it up; it lights the grass on fire for about 50 feet behind you," Rick said. Rick went on to explain that jet engines are not like car engines, they don't need gears to make them go fast. They just push constantly with 60 pounds of thrust, and you keep going faster and faster until you turn them off or hit something. "Oh by the way, the brakes are worthless," Rick said. I told him, I thought I would wait till he got the bugs worked out.

The next time I stopped by I asked about the rocket bike. "I had to take it apart and get rid of it," Rick said, "every damn fool daredevil in the county wanted to ride it. They stole it out of the barn and took it for a joyride in the dark one night. I was afraid someone would get killed!"

I sure wish I would have taken a picture of that thing, but it was so scary I was glad to see it was gone!

Blow the Bridge

Standing on a piece of ¾ plywood above the bed of a borrowed pick up truck, I was grinding away rock on a lion's head restoring the north pallister of the Foster Park bridge. The damage had occurred many years ago when the river flooded. A newspaper article reported the bridge washed away and was later raised higher when it was replaced.

I had a small generator roaring away in the truck bed to make power for my diamond faced grinding tool. The lion was ten feet off the ground and I was replacing the rock broken off its face.

I noticed a man in uniform walking across the bridge. He came down and stood by the tailgate of the truck and looked like he wanted to talk. I needed a little break anyway so I shut off my tool and the generator, took off my goggles, face mask and ear muffs and said, "Howdy, what can I do for you my friend?"

He said," I'm Drew Mashburn, the park ranger here, and I met a guy that told me his Dad blew this bridge up." My first thought was, it sounds like the guy was missing a few cookies.

I said, "Hey that's great, why did he do that?"

Drew said the guy told him, "There was a big storm back in 1938. It only flooded in the Ventura river north. This river was in full flood stage, flowing bank to bank, with trees and brush rolling down. Debris started piling up against the bridge. The water behind the log jam was rising and began to flood the houses in Foster Park.

Back then, you could buy dynamite at the hardware store for blowing stumps or rocks, and his dad had about 40 sticks in his garage. He sloshed down here in the pouring rain and climbed up under the flooded abutment, setting 20 sticks with waterproof fuse, lit it and took off running. The forthcoming explosion did the trick, the bridge broke loose and the log jam washed away, saving the town.

I said, "Wow that's amazing, what a hero!"

He said," No one saw him do it, everyone took off when it started to flood and he never said anything about it because he thought he might get arrested for blowing it up."

We talked for a little while longer, and as he walked away he said, "The kids would sit on these lions and wait for the train to take them to school in the morning." (How cool is that!) I thanked him for the great stories, started my generator and got back to work. The insight into the history really helped me focus on my repair job on the lion's head.

I was grinding away, when out of the corner of my eye I saw something running across the bridge. It was a teenaged Texas longhorn tri-color cow, loose! She galloped by, like the wind, and was headed for the freeway. I threw down my grinder, jumped in the truck with the generator still running and caught her about half way up the on ramp. Lucky for everyone, she turned around and ran back down and under the freeway overpass. I backed up and took off after her again. She was headed for the coast on old highway 33. I ran her up a fenced side road with a gate. And thought I had her cornered, but she got down on her knees and crawled under the barbed wire fence into a pasture full of cows. I sat there for a while watching her and suddenly realized my generator was still running and tipped over on its side in the back of the truck.

When I finally got back to the Foster Park bridge, I decided that I had all the excitement I could stand for one day and headed for home.

Hammer Man

When I was young, there were amazing people all around me and watching them changed my life. I didn't understand what the words meant, when I read books. So most of my early learning came from seeing. A huge statue in downtown Seattle of a man swinging a hammer, brought back memories of an old friend. It was a fitting tribute to Marvin, the real hammer man.

I was working with a contractor as a carpenter on the remodel of the old Smith-Hobson estate. We were turning it into the new Ojai City Hall. They put me to work on demolition and cutting holes in the lathe and plaster for new doorways.

There was an African-American man who seemed to be everywhere on the job site. Marvin was about 60 years old and a whirlwind of a carpenter. He could do more in a day than four people. He had years of experience and knew the fastest, easiest way to do everything. He wasn't in a hurry, he just made every move count.

Whenever I could, I would keep my eye on Marvin. I learned so much just watching him. In one day he cut, bent and staked the 60 foot curvy sidewalk down between the round cement pillars of the trellis walkway leading into the city hall. It would have taken me a week to do that. Then he poured and trowled it the next day. It was stripped before he left to go to another job late that afternoon. He was there the next morning hanging doors when I got to work.

Marvin was making about two dollars an hour more than I was. I thought they should have been paying him $100 an hour but he was just glad to have some work. He was a superstar carpenter, like watching Magic Johnson play basketball.

One day when he was performing some other miracle, he noticed there was something wrong with his hammer, it wasn't working very well. I should have been working too, but I was standing there watching him instead. I went over to see what was wrong. Marvin showed me his hammer and the whole end with the head on it was worn off!

Now to this day I have never seen anybody wear the head off a hammer. Marvin told me that when they sold it to him, it had a lifetime guarantee. Our boss thought it was amazing too. He got on the phone and called Stanley Tools and told them that Marvin's hammer was worn out. He was told it was supposed to last a lifetime, would they please bring him a new one. Everybody thought it was funny, except Marvin.

Sure enough, about an hour later a Stanley Tool truck showed up on the job site and gave Marvin a brand new hammer! They took the old hammer to show their boss. I wish I could have kept that hammer, it was an amazing thing to see a worn out claw hammer. That's why we called Marvin, 'The Hammer Man.' He taught me how to work!

June Bugs

Who would be knocking on the back door this late? I opened the door and out in the dark stood my friend Dinosaur Dave. He said, "I'm going to gather some June bugs for my Koi, do you want to come?"

"It's two A.M. why so late ?" I asked.

"Because that's when they are out" Dave replied.
It was a warm summer night and it sounded like fun so I said, "ok". Dave gave me a paper sandwich bag to hold my catch and we were off.

"Where do June bugs gather?" I asked.

"You can find them around any outdoor light at night," says Dave, "but the best place to find them is under the street lights. They are attracted to the big lights but there is nowhere for them to land, and they get tired and fall to the pavement. All we have to do is pick them up."

Sure enough, under nearly every street light, we gathered six or seven nice big June bugs. I was a little spooked as I picked up my first one, (they are about three inches long around here).They seem like they might bite, but you just grab them real quick and throw them in the sack. After a while, the noise of them scratching on the paper bag trying to get out, got pretty loud.Thirty bugs can make some real noise. It was strange holding a paper bag full of June bugs, they were heavy, so I helped Dinosaur Dave carry them back to his house. I told him thanks for a great adventure and headed on back to my shop.

On my way home I heard a chain link fence rattling and stopped to investigate. In the dim light off of someone's back porch, I saw something climbing the fence. As it jumped down I caught sight of a big long tail. It was a mountain lion! I hurried home looking over my shoulder.

The Fire Truck

Mathew's young son, who was having a birthday soon, had been considering becoming a fireman. Mat went out searching for a nice toy fire truck for him. The only truck he could find was poorly made and priced well over one hundred dollars, so he decided to keep on looking.

Out and about one day, he stopped by an estate sale of one of his father's friends. They had old cars, trucks and tractors parked all over a big field out behind the barn. The ranch owner had died recently and they were getting rid of his collection of treasures. Mat noticed something red in the back row and went out to see what it was. It was a 1937 Reo fire truck without an engine or transmission. When he asked how much, the owner said, $300 so Mat bought it and hauled it home.

On his son's birthday he gave it to the young future fireman, but It took Mat most of the afternoon to convince his young son that the fire truck actually belonged to him!

The Freezer

He was stuck in traffic on the freeway when a small quiet voice spoke to him. It said, "Make a sled, get some dogs, drive across the Canadian arctic and happiness will find you!

When he told me this story I was skeptical, but over a period of two years, he made a pretty nice, arctic dog sled. Most of his free time was spent teaching a bunch of rescued malamutes how to pull a wheel cart around in the beach sand.

The whole project still looked a little iffy to me. That's a long way on the ice by yourself, even if you are a 6' 5" fearless Norwegian. After all the abuse, the eskimos might not be friendly. How are you going to feed your dogs? Many questions were left unanswered as he loaded up and flew off to Alaska in the middle of winter.

After landing in Barrow, he packed his sled and slid off across the ice, heading east. His first few days were tough, getting the dogs acclimated and working together, learning about snow and ice. It was all new to him but he stayed right with it. Everything went okay till the first big storm hit. The wind blew a four day white out and he ran out of food for the dogs. Fortunately they were attacked by a polar bear which he managed to kill for meat.

He was moving along slowly one morning when he saw a half buried snowmobile off in the distance. As he got closer his dogs started barking and a gloved hand came up out of the snow. He jumped off his sled and dug the eskimo out . The old man had run out of gas and was nearly dead from exposure. He put the man on his sled with a warm huskie and took him to the next village nearly 50 miles away. As they traveled and camped, the eskimo slowly came back to life, just in time for their arrival.

Although my friend couldn't understand the language, he was amazed at the reception they received. It was a big deal bringing the old man in. Before this day my friend was just another wannabe dog sledder on his own journey, but suddenly his whole life changed forever. One of the eskimo spoke english. He was told, the man he saved from freezing to death was the most important native inuit shaman alive, and the spirits must have sent my friend here to save his life.

There was a huge party and people came from near and far to celebrate. Sled man was given an eskimo name, new dogs and new winter clothes made of caribou skins and wolf fur. He also received food for many days and special amulets to keep him safe on his long journey. Word of what he had done preceded him all the way across the northern arctic and everywhere he went he was treated like a great old friend and a hero. He made it all the way to Greenland before returning.

When he got back he told me this story, and when I asked him what he was going to do now, he said, "I'm going back where I belong," and I haven't seen him since.

Big Pig

It's nice to have friends that manage a large part of an island. Once in a while they take a vacation and need someone to island-sit while they are gone. More than once, Hugh and I got invited to come over and keep an eye on the east end of Santa Cruz island. They would fly us out to the hill, with our food and gear above scorpion bay. It took two passes. The first pass was to scare the animals away from the landing strip, and the second pass was to land. From there it was about a mile across the island to smugglers cove where we ate and slept.

Back then the island was full of Merino sheep and feral hogs. There were also horses, small kit foxes, lots of birds and an occasional pirate or two. What a fine place to have all to yourself for a couple of weeks. I remember being amazed at the peace and quiet, except for the bleat of sheep or the grunt of a rooting hog.

There was no electricity and kerosene lamps provided light. By day we fished for our dinner and then went exploring the many hidden canyons all around our deserted island retreat. We would get up with the sun and sit on ocean facing cliffs and watch pods of gray whales swimming by. There were large flocks of pelicans feeding on huge upwelling schools of anchovies being attacked from below by dolphins. The sea gulls would sweep down and try to steal fish out of the pelican's beaks. Hugh said he felt sorry for the pelicans; they dove down and did all the work and the gulls just came and robbed them. He said he felt like he was a pelican and that's what the world had done to him. (When he died several years later, I carved a pelican and hollowed it out to put his ashes in.)

On rainy days we built fires in the riverbed out of eucalyptus branches and ate like kings while Hugh talked about the good old days. We had fresh caught red snapper, shrimp and crab with steamed veggies and leg of lamb. After dinner we read the history of Santa Cruz Island, and the shipwreck book out loud. One of the things I really liked to do by myself in the evening was climb up rainbow ridge and watch the lights on the mainland come on. It was like being an Indian witness to the new world.

One night I stayed a little too long and noticed it was getting really dark. As I started down the trail, I could barely make out which way to go. The dirt trail was a little lighter than the surrounding brush, and my eyes began to adjust as I got away from the lights on the coast. Farther down the hill, I heard some sticks breaking close by and stopped to see what was making all the noise. From out of the brush something came pushing through the purple thistle. It was moving slowly. A huge black shadow moved out into the dry grass and stopped and looked right at me. I'm 6'2" and it was waist high to me, and at least twelve feet long. It looked like a short legged hippopotamus. Then it grunted and I realized it was a huge black pig. It stood there for a long moment, started chewing on something, and moved back into the deep brush breaking branches as it went. I didn't know pigs got that big!

After that, I found other things to do after dark…

Sergio's Transformation

Java n' Joe's was the place to be when three o'clock rolled around. All sorts of Ojai's odd characters would put their tools, telephones, pencils and brushes up to congregate for a cup of coffee and a chat as the day wound down.

Just around the corner and upstairs, Sergio Aragones had his studio. He was a cartoonist for MAD magazine and worked at night. He would come over for coffee before going up to start drawing. It was fun to watch him illustrate the conversations as they were spoken. I have piles of pictures drawn on old newspapers or napkins, whatever was available at the moment. Other times we would sit outside or whittle on spoons. Sergio liked to make little snakes out of the wooden stir sticks. It was a wonderful gathering before I went for my evening walk.

It was around this time that John Nava got a commission from the Catholic Archdiocese to paint all the saints for the new Our Lady Of The Angels Catholic cathedral down in Los Angeles. John needed models and most of them were people from Ojai. The paintings would be sewn into silk tapestries 12 feet tall to hang around the inside of the huge chapel. It was fun to hear about who got chosen to be which saint. Sergio was picked to be Saint Jude and I thought that was pretty cool. When Sergio got back from modeling he told me, "John wants you to be Saint Patrick." Wow what a thrill!

I showed up for my appointment a few days later in clean pants and a nice shirt that Denny Miller gave me. I sat in John's studio for a while waiting for the woman who handled the wardrobe. Her name was Cyrena and she was wonderful. She took my shirt and put me in the nicest linen undergarment I had ever put on, then helped me into the beautiful hand embroidered silk bishop's robe. Next came the green silk, shoulder to floor overcaller. It was hand embroidered with golden thread crosses. I was ready for my closeup. He had me look at a spot high on the wall and took pictures of my face, hands and bare feet. John said I had great hands to paint so I held them wide and low. (Everyone else clasped their hands in prayer). When it was all over, I realized how comfortable it was to wear such fine robes. I could get used to this. I asked my wardrobe lady if I could keep the robes. The answer was a very pleasant "no."

A couple of weeks later we were sitting having afternoon coffee at Java n' Joe's, when a lovely young woman came by and stopped to chat. Sergio with his quick and wonderful wit told her, "We would love to tell you what a beautiful woman you are but we can't. We're all saints!"

Mc Andrew's Ghost

Mc Andrew was a scotsman, and when he first arrived he had a considerable amount of money. He liked it here and decided to settle down and buy some land. Unfortunately he wasn't a farmer, it seemed like everything he did failed. The farm froze in the winter, died in the drought or he (being quite thrifty) bought the wrong variety because it was cheaper and no one wanted his crop. Eventually he ran out of money and had to sell some of his land to make ends meet. As he got older, the neighbors built houses all around him and he only had the small lot under his own house left. He became a grumpy old coot that nobody liked and died alone and lonely. The people that bought his house claimed it was haunted. Sometimes late at night they would hear his ghost moving around, groaning.

I was on my way up the hill before dawn one morning to walk, when I spotted something white floating across the road. The first thing that came to mind was Mc Andrew's ghost. It must be him out looking at his former land wishing he had never sold it. As I got a little closer, I realized it was a black bear carrying a white plastic bag full of trash. It turned out to be a great time to remind myself not to believe everything I think!

Ba Boom

Way back when the space shuttles still flew, I got word that Columbia was going to land at Edwards Air Force Base the next day. I dug out my map and saw that the flight path took it right over Pine Mountain summit, near where I live. I loaded up my old VW van, chugged up highway 33 to the turn off of Pine Mountain Rd. and drove to the campgrounds. It was a weekday so the place was empty.

I built a fire, made some dinner and went to bed, hoping to get a glimpse of the spaceship as it whistled over early the next morning. The views from the mountaintop were breathtaking. I was sitting on a rock outcropping as the sun came up, looking west for some sign of my spaceship when the powerful double sonic boom hit! Quite suddenly the whole place shook and there were tree limbs and pine cones raining down all over the top of the mountain. From out of nowhere bears came clamoring out of holes in the rock, trotting around in a panic. A herd of frightened deer galloped back and forth over the top of the mountain fleeing the falling debris. Raven flew around cawing to each other. Terrified squirrels scampered up and down the monstrous Jeffrey pines chirping their fears. The morning was like something from outer space.

It took me a moment to realize what had just happened. The space shuttle had gone over me faster than the speed of sound (720 MPH) and when the huge sonic Ba Boom hit it was already many miles past and gone. It took twenty minutes for the debris to stop falling and everything to settle back down. I sat there stunned for a long time and didn't realize my mouth was open, till I swallowed a bug..............................BA BOOM!

(If I tried to write ba boom as loud as it was it would be 10 feet tall and 25 feet long)

Whoa Boy

My old friend Cam stopped and showed me a reel of Joaquin, another young friend, riding a bucking bronco in a rodeo. It was amazing. The horse was really animated. After getting pitched in every direction imaginable, Joaquin stepped off like it was a walk in the park.

Cam had been a cowboy all his life and he knew a lot about horses. Being the head wrangler at Thacher school for thirty years, he taught at least a thousand people how to ride a horse. I hadn't considered all that when I started telling him what I thought about his movie. It looks to me like he's not taking enough time to get to know his horse. Maybe he should walk his horse around a little bit, brush him down and give him a few horse cookies. That might help calm him down. Those horses can get a little testy if you don't show them enough respect.

Cam said, "Yes I've had that happen to me too. When it does, I just tell them, 'whoa boy, whoa boy,' over and over. Usually it doesn't help, but it makes me feel better."

Then I said, "When they really get to bucking, it's hard to tell which end you're talking to. Maybe the horse didn't hear everything you said."

We both laughed and Cam said, "I think you're right." As I was leaving, he said, "You have a great day, but if it goes to bucking, just yell 'whoa boy, whoa boy'."

The Boathouse Shower

My friend was Irish and a military veteran that played a mean piano. His initials were D.O.C. So that's what I called him, DOC.

I practiced my sand sculptures at the San Simeon cove before the 4th of July contest at Cayucos. That's where I got to know him. He had a kayak rental business at the cove for several years. His customers would complain about having to rinse off in cold water, so he snuck in a 40 gallon electric water heater with the faucets and shower head sticking out through the wall. DOC would let me park my VW van next to his building overnight whenever I came up to visit. It was nice for me, I had a private campsite with a hot shower. The building where he kept his kayaks was an old garage with a small office down near the pier. My job was to keep an eye on the place at night.

It was late January and there was talk of big weather coming with a six foot storm surge and huge seas likely. Lucky me, I got there just before it came ashore. It was a maritime polar with a tropical fetch that gave it warm heavy rains to accompany its cold winter winds. The kind of storm that is every sea captain's worst nightmare, but lucky me, I was ashore. The sun was down when the leading edge came over with powerful winds and driving rain. I checked to make sure no trees were going to fall on me and climbed in my van and listened to the roar of the sea. The winds and rain finally rocked me to sleep. I woke up several times but it was too dark and nasty to see anything.

With the light of dawn peaking in, I sat up and put on my rain gear. Timidly sliding the door open, I stepped out into the howling winds and pounding rain. I looked out at the unbelievable scene. The waves were monstrous, 25 to 30 feet high. They broke as they came around the point about a half mile away. Then they reformed again. The waves came in to break a second time, in gigantic long tubes to crash like visible thunder 15 feet high on the beach just below me, sending white water blasting all the way across the parking lot and smashing into the stone cliff. Huge waves then bashing off the rocks headed back out to sea to crash head on into the incoming waves sounding very much like sonic booms, sending spray 20 feet higher than the 30 foot pier nearby.

As the waves in the shorebreak passed underneath the pier pilings,10 foot high fans of seawater sprayed from the cracks between the boards of the pier deck making an amazing rapid fire slapping sound to go along with the roar of the tumbling bashing seas. The beachfront was full of driftwood washing out from the overflowing creek nearby and being picked up by the mountainous breakers to be crushed against the cliffs and the pier adding to the amazing sights. There were seagulls and pelicans trying to fly in the freezing, gusting winds when I noticed a splash of peach underneath the deep dark, Payne's gray clouds of the storm blowing by. I felt myself getting wet and cold in the raging wind. I turned around and noticed the handles and shower head sticking out of the wall beside me. I peeled off my wet clothes and tossed them in the open door of my van and turned on the hot water. It felt so good as I stepped into the spray.

I was standing there in the cold blasting winds and rain, as warm as I could be, seeing the most wonderful display of Mother Nature in all her wildest fury. I washed my hair, shaved and watched in total amazement until I realized I had run completely out of hot water. It was without a doubt the finest shower I have ever taken. Thank you, DOC.

Cover painting illustrated by Dennis Shives, inspired by a story called 'I Don't Believe It' from the book entitled "More True Stories to Read Aloud."

Made in the USA
Middletown, DE
16 March 2022

62685028R00057